GW01458347

Ceramics Industry Advisory Committee

Safe operation of ceramic kilns

HSE BOOKS

ISBN 0 7176 0630 9

Contents

Foreword *v*

Introduction *1*
Legislation *1*
Scope *1*

Types of kiln *1*
Intermittent kilns *1*
Continuous kilns *2*
Fast fire kilns *2*

Training of kiln operators *2*

Natural gas and other gaseous fuel-fired kilns *3*
General *3*
Liquefied petroleum gas *3*
Mine drainage and land-fill gas *3*
Common features of all gaseous fuel supply systems *3*
Ignition *3*
Air supplies *4*
Ventilation of combustion products *4*
Safety controls *7*
Operating procedures *10*
Explosion relief *10*

Electric kilns *10*
Statutory requirements *10*
Interlocking *12*
Precautions for intermittent kilns *12*
Precautions for continuous kilns *13*
Precautions for fast fire kilns *14*

Maintenance of plant and safety equipment *14*
Health risks *14*

Fires and the siting of pottery kilns *15*
Remedial measures *15*

Thermal environment *16*
Remedial measures *17*

Other considerations *17*
Means of access *17*
Mechanical hazards *17*
Ergonomic factors *17*
Lighting *18*
Noise *18*
Fumes from kilns *18*

Appendix 1   EC requirements and British Standards   *19*

Appendix 2   Training requirements for kiln operators   *20*

Appendix 3   Application of programmable electronic systems to fuel burners   *21*

Appendix 4   Suggested content of kiln maintenance record   *23*

Appendix 5   Calculation of heat stress and thermal comfort   *24*

References   *25*

FOREWORD

This booklet was produced by the Ceramics Industry
Advisory Committee which was set up in 1977 by the
Health and Safety Commission to advise on the
protection of people at work from hazards to health and
safety arising from their occupation within the ceramics
industry. The Committee is composed of equal numbers
of employer and trade union representatives and is
assisted by advisers from the Health and Safety
Executive.

The Health and Safety Commission has endorsed the
practical guidance contained in this document, which it
commends to the ceramics industry.

INTRODUCTION

1   Ceramic kilns are essentially simple and safe to use provided that the proper controls and safety devices are fitted and that the safe method of working is fully understood, both by management and kiln operators. The Ceramics Industry Advisory Committee (CIAC) is concerned that clear practical guidance on safe operation and current good practice should be available to the industry.

2   It is acknowledged that technological developments can lead to significant changes in recognised safety devices and precautions. Their exclusion from this booklet does not therefore necessarily mean that they are unacceptable. As a general test, any method or device used should achieve at least an equivalent standard of safety as the recommendations set out here. If there is any doubt about the suitability of these alternative methods or devices, advice may be obtained from a competent person, eg the fuel or equipment supplier or from the Health and Safety Executive.

3   Workers have been killed and property badly damaged in explosions caused through the ignition of unburnt fuel in gas-fired kilns. Gassing by the carbon monoxide produced from incompletely burnt fuel also presents a serious risk, as do spillages of liquefied petroleum products used as fuels. With electric kilns, there is danger of electrocution, electric shock and burn injuries from heating elements and other conductors.

Legislation

4   The Health and Safety at Work etc Act 1974[1] imposes duties on employers, employees and also manufacturers of equipment for use at work. In addition to this, the Management of Health and Safety at Work Regulations 1992[2] require employers to assess risks in the workplace and ensure that appropriate precautions are being taken; also to make sure that employees have adequate health and safety training and are capable enough at their jobs to avoid risks. The Workplace (Health, Safety and Welfare) Regulations 1992[3] are concerned with the working environment as a whole. They apply in full to new workplaces now and to existing workplaces from 1996. These will be referred to later in this booklet. Other Regulations[4], including the Provision and Use of Work Equipment Regulations 1992[5], apply specifically to the safety standards of equipment and machinery. Certain standards are particularly relevant to ceramic kilns, including EC pr EN 746, *Industrial thermoprocessing equipment* [6], and British Gas Code of Practice IM 30, *The use of gas in industrial process plant 1993*[7].

5   Information about European Community policy on the status of standards and codes of practice is given in Appendix 1.

Scope

6   This booklet provides guidance on suitable standards of installation for natural gas-fired, other gaseous fuel-fired and electric kilns. Intermittent and continuous kilns, including those of massive construction and the more modern fast fire type are included. Related topics such as training of operators, plant maintenance, thermal environment, kiln siting and mechanical hazards are also covered. It revises and expands the booklet on kiln safety produced in 1977 by the Joint Standing Committee for the Pottery and Allied Industries which the Ceramics Industry Advisory Committee replaced. Information is not included on liquid fuel-fired kilns as there are no known major users in the industry.

TYPES OF KILN

7   There are a number of different types of ceramic kiln, which vary in their size, construction and mode of operation. The following are the main ones, but it is recognised that there are others with combined features such as roller hearth kilns, as well as more specialised types.

Intermittent kilns

8   Intermittent kilns are heated up and cooled down frequently, typically every day. There are various different types:

(a)   *small bench mounted top or front-loading kilns -* which may be similar in shape and size to a domestic oven and are loaded with trays of ware by hand. These are used particularly in schools and colleges, but also factories, and for experimental purposes in laboratories. When used in educational establishments, the construction of such kilns may be subject to guidance laid down by the local education authority. These would usually be electric;

(b)   *larger oven-type kilns -* are similar in principle to (a) above, but are usually loaded by pushing a pre-loaded truck of ware into them on rails; and

(c)   *lift-cover or 'top-hat' and moving-cover kilns -* in which the kiln cover is put over a pre-loaded stillage of ware. Both cover and base are usually fitted with heating elements, in the case of electric

1

kilns. For gas kilns, the burners are fitted in the cover with flexible gas connections. A variation of this type of kiln has the cover fixed with the base carrying the ware rising into the kiln.

Continuous kilns

9   These are also known as tunnel kilns by virtue of their construction. Traditionally made of brick, these kilns are maintained at working temperature for several months at a time. The ware is loaded on trucks which are automatically propelled through the tunnel at a very slow speed.

Fast fire kilns

10   These are now commonly seen in many larger potteries. They combine design features and production advantages of both intermittent and continuous kilns. Ware is usually placed in a single layer on refractory bats and transported by a conveyor system along a compact tunnel of low thermal mass. With heating up periods taking as little as an hour, they would usually be fired daily.

TRAINING OF KILN OPERATORS

11   It should be appreciated that most safety devices on ceramic kilns are intended to deal only with temporary deviations from normal operating conditions, such as an interruption in the fuel supply. These devices are not a substitute for proper care and attention in operating kilns. An important safeguard against accidents is an conscientious and well trained operator, available at all times.

12   Only a person authorised by management should be permitted to operate a kiln. Before authorisation, employees should be thoroughly trained in the safe operation of the kiln and, for gas kilns, be provided with comprehensive light-up and shut-down instructions. The instructions issued by the kiln manufacturer for the individual kiln on which the operator is to work should form the basis of training. Guidance on the topics which should be covered can be found in Appendix 2. Periodic refresher training at intervals not greater than five years should also be provided.

Figure 1   Modern fast fire kiln

NATURAL GAS AND OTHER GASEOUS FUEL-FIRED KILNS

General

13 In order that all kilns fired by natural gas and other gaseous fuels may be operated safely, certain minimum requirements are necessary. With modern developments in kiln technology, safety standards need to be set with reference to the **frequency** with which the kiln is lit rather than its structure. Separate consideration needs to be given to continuous kilns of massive construction which operate for long periods of time (several months) at high temperatures (see paragraphs 55 and 56).

14 There are a number of specific regulations[8], British Standards and codes of practice which cover gas installations. Some of these are listed at the end of this document. If there is any doubt as to which of these are relevant in any particular circumstances, the advice of British Gas or the gas supplier, if different, should be sought.

15 Generally speaking, most gas-fired kilns are supplied with natural gas from the gas main. Occasionally, they may use gas supplied from a mine gas drainage system, land-fill gas or liquefied petroleum gas (LPG).

Liquefied petroleum gas

16 Special consideration needs to be given to the safe storage of LPG. Guidance on bulk storage in fixed tanks can be found in the HSE Guidance Booklet HS(G) 34[9]. In small potteries, where LPG is supplied from cylinders, safety guidelines can be found in the HSE Guidance Note CS4[10]. If neat butane is used with a trace heated pipeline system, a warning device in the pipeline system to operate in the event of low butane temperature, should be provided.

17 In the areas beneath and around plant using LPG as a fuel, particular care should be exercised to avoid any unventilated low-level pits, gullies, voids or tunnels as its denser-than-air properties may cause dangerous accumulations of gas.

18 Vents and filling points should not be sited near cellars, pits, ducts etc. Where there is any risk of explosion due to the collection of gas from spilt fuel, electrical equipment and wiring should be excluded or be of an explosion-protected type. Advice is given in BS 5345: 1987 (IP Code)[11].

Mine drainage and land-fill gas

19 The Firedamp Drainage Regulations 1960[12]

govern the use of gas from mines' drainage systems and require that a producer of mine gas should ensure that the gas has a minimum volume of 40% methane. Mains natural gas may be added to maintain this level. No additional safety features over and above those required for natural gas are necessary. However, where LPG is stored to augment the calorific value of the mine drainage gas, this will need special considerations (see paragraph 16).

20 Where land-fill gas is used, special attention may need to be given to the variability of supply and possible corrosion of pipes and fittings.

Common features of all gaseous fuel supply systems

21 The following parts of gaseous systems are not covered in detail in this booklet as specific guidance is given in British Gas Code of Practice IM 30:

(a) isolation valves;

(b) filters;

(c) pressure control devices (including pressure switches and non-return valves);

(d) flexible pipework;

(e) vents;

(f) throughput and fuel/air ratio controls; and

(g) air/gas mixing machines.

22 Safety shut-off valves are covered under the section headed Safety controls (paragraphs 42 to 45).

Ignition

23 It should be possible for one person to light the burners. A source of ignition should be provided for their smooth and reliable ignition. Where reasonably practicable, automatic or semi-automatic ignition systems, which comply with the intent of BS 5885[13] and which incorporate kiln pre-purge, ignition and flame test, should be provided (see paragraph 52 for fuller details). There should additionally be a post-run purge, to remove any residual gas from inside the kiln.

24 Gas should not be supplied to any burner before the source of ignition has been actuated and an adequate purge carried out.

25 Where observation ports are provided, they should be arranged so that the operator has a clear view of the

pilot and main burners from a safe, easily accessible position.

26   Burner ignition should be accomplished by:

(a)   ignition of a fixed and properly located pilot burner and subsequent ignition of the main burner; or

(b)   direct ignition of the main burner at low-fire flow rate.

27   Where reasonably practicable, lighting torches should be replaced by automatic, or semi-automatic ignition systems, as described in paragraph 52. If torches are to be retained, the system should have the following features:

(a)   the ignition port should be positioned to ensure smooth and reliable ignition of the main burner;

(b)   supplies to lighting torches should be designed so that they cannot be inadvertently left on, eg by the use of interlocked or timed solenoid valves. The supply of gas to the torch should not be possible until after the kiln purge period. Gas torches should be extinguished and removed immediately after use;

(c)   **ignition should take place with the kiln door open;**

(d)   operators should be specifically trained in the correct method of lighting up;

(e)   written light-up instructions should be available near to the kiln.

28   Lighting torches should be stable under all operating conditions. They should be unaffected by pressure fluctuations on burner light-up, variations in kiln chamber pressure, or draught from burner combustion air.

29   If a main flame does not ignite **within five seconds**, then the gas supply to the main burner should be shut off immediately and the lighting torch removed and turned off. The kiln should then be purged with a volume of air, or left for a period of time sufficient to disperse any accumulation of unburnt gas before a second ignition sequence is started.

30   Multiple burners should be lit separately and in a predetermined order compatible with the plant design; the first flame should be properly established before the second flame is ignited and be unaffected by ignition of the second flame, and so on, in sequence.

If light-up problems persist beyond the normal light-up time, advice should be sought from another competent person. As a general rule, **not more than three attempts** to light any burner should be made before seeking help.

31   Diagrams illustrating ignition sequences for gas-fired kilns are shown in Figures 2 and 3.

32   Where sparking plugs with high voltage flexible leads are used for ignition, there should be an individual electrical supply, lead and spark plug for each burner. The electrical equipment should be suitably designed to prevent accidental contact with dangerous live parts and the sparking plug connector provided with adequate insulation. The switches should be of the type that are spring-returned to the off position.

Air supplies

33   In order to dilute to a safe concentration any residual flammable vapours, the kiln should have a pre-ignition purge with at least five times the kiln's volume of air. This can normally be achieved by operating induced and forced-draught fans for the length of time specified in the operating instructions before allowing any fuel valves to be opened. On kilns relying on chimneys and natural draught, the flammability of the gases in the kiln should, where reasonably practicable, be checked and light-up should not proceed until the concentration of flammable gas has reached a safe level, ie <25% of the lower explosive limit. With this type of kiln, this can be achieved by leaving the door(s) standing open before, during and after light-up.

34   Where long pre-ignition purge periods are unacceptable between normal plant operations, consideration should be given to enhanced proving of the safety shut-off system at and during shutdown.

35   The ventilation of the building and plant should allow an adequate supply of combustion air to reach the burner(s) under all conditions.

36   Further guidance is given in the British Gas Code of Practice IM 30.

Ventilation of combustion products

37   Correct draught conditions should be maintained at all times, so as to remove unwanted products of combustion, and to avoid down draughts. It should be possible to obtain and maintain a stable draught under all operational conditions.

38   The flue for a kiln should not be connected to flues used for other purposes and there should preferably be

Figure 2 Ignition sequence for gas-fired kilns with automatic or semi-automatic ignition and flame safeguards

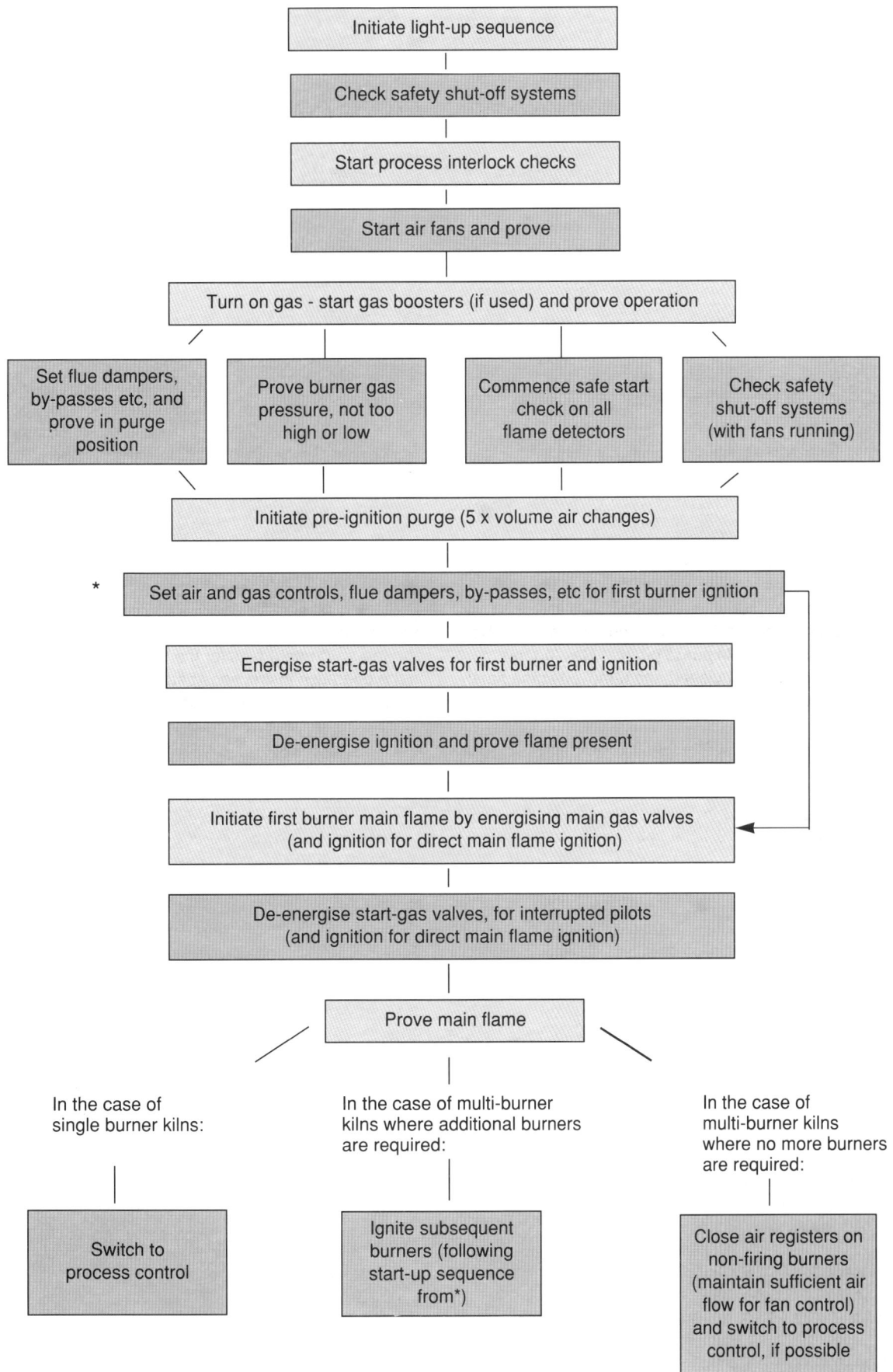

```
                    ┌─────────────────────────────────┐
                    │    Initiate light-up sequence    │
                    └─────────────────────────────────┘
                                    │
                    ┌─────────────────────────────────┐
                    │   Check safety shut-off systems  │
                    └─────────────────────────────────┘
                                    │
                    ┌─────────────────────────────────┐
                    │   Start process interlock checks │
                    └─────────────────────────────────┘
                                    │
                    ┌─────────────────────────────────┐
                    │       Start air fans and prove   │
                    └─────────────────────────────────┘
                                    │
        ┌───────────────────────────────────────────────────────────┐
        │ Turn on gas - start gas boosters (if used) and prove operation │
        └───────────────────────────────────────────────────────────┘
```

| Set flue dampers, by-passes etc, and prove in purge position | Prove burner gas pressure, not too high or low | Commence safe start check on all flame detectors | Check safety shut-off systems (with fans running) |

```
        ┌───────────────────────────────────────────────────────────┐
        │   Initiate pre-ignition purge (5 x volume air changes)    │
        └───────────────────────────────────────────────────────────┘
                                    │
    *   ┌───────────────────────────────────────────────────────────┐
        │ Set air and gas controls, flue dampers, by-passes, etc for first burner ignition │
        └───────────────────────────────────────────────────────────┘
                                    │
        ┌───────────────────────────────────────────────────────────┐
        │  Energise start-gas valves for first burner and ignition  │
        └───────────────────────────────────────────────────────────┘
                                    │
        ┌───────────────────────────────────────────────────────────┐
        │      De-energise ignition and prove flame present         │
        └───────────────────────────────────────────────────────────┘
                                    │
        ┌───────────────────────────────────────────────────────────┐
        │ Initiate first burner main flame by energising main gas valves │
        │   (and ignition for direct main flame ignition)           │
        └───────────────────────────────────────────────────────────┘
                                    │
        ┌───────────────────────────────────────────────────────────┐
        │ De-energise start-gas valves, for interrupted pilots      │
        │   (and ignition for direct main flame ignition)           │
        └───────────────────────────────────────────────────────────┘
                                    │
                    ┌─────────────────────────────────┐
                    │        Prove main flame          │
                    └─────────────────────────────────┘
```

In the case of single burner kilns:	In the case of multi-burner kilns where additional burners are required:	In the case of multi-burner kilns where no more burners are required:
Switch to process control	Ignite subsequent burners (following start-up sequence from*)	Close air registers on non-firing burners (maintain sufficient air flow for fan control) and switch to process control, if possible

Figure 3 Ignition sequence for gas-fired kilns with manual ignition systems and no flame safeguard devices (see paragraph 55)

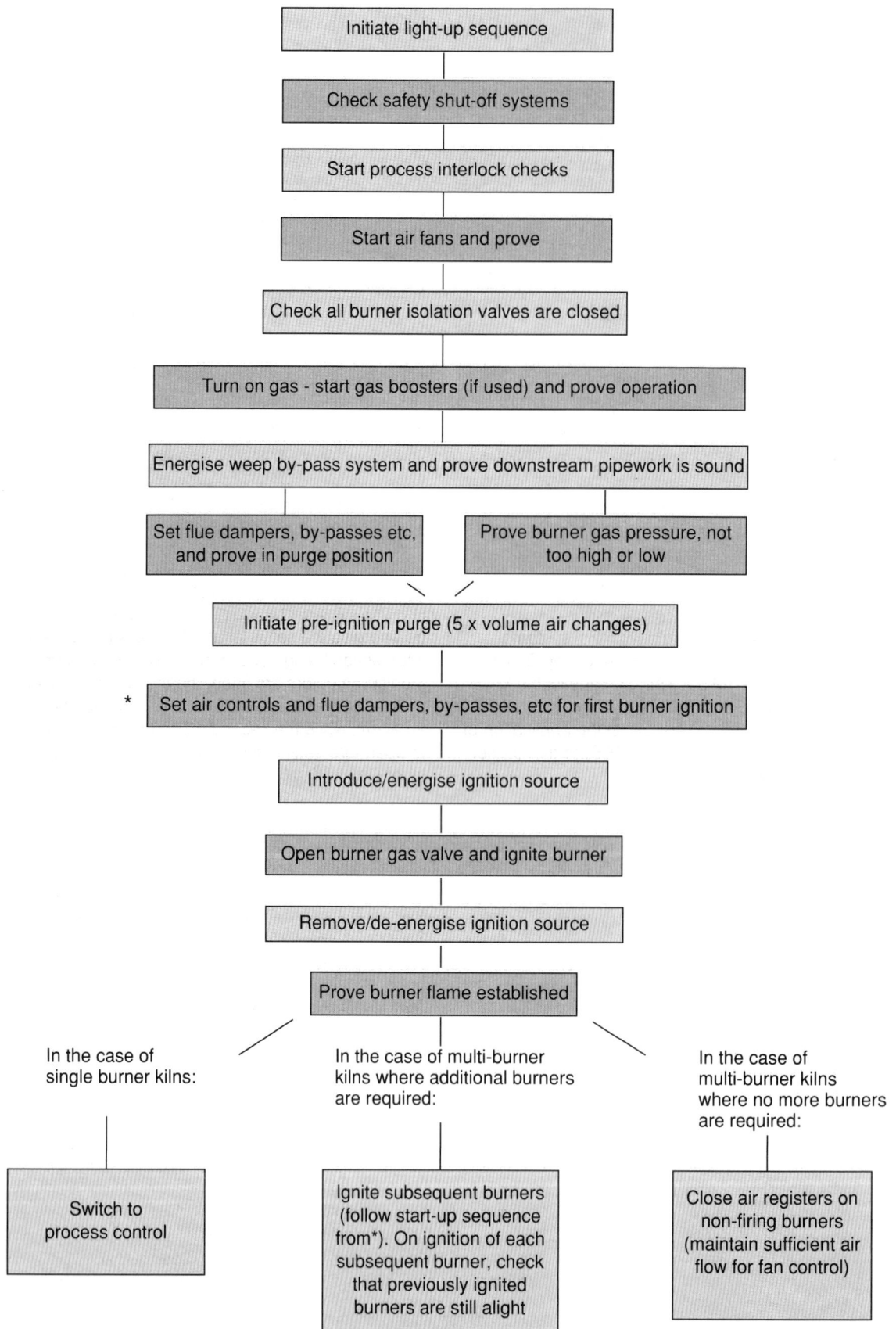

```
┌─────────────────────────────────────────┐
│         Initiate light-up sequence        │
└─────────────────────────────────────────┘
                    │
┌─────────────────────────────────────────┐
│        Check safety shut-off systems      │
└─────────────────────────────────────────┘
                    │
┌─────────────────────────────────────────┐
│        Start process interlock checks     │
└─────────────────────────────────────────┘
                    │
┌─────────────────────────────────────────┐
│           Start air fans and prove        │
└─────────────────────────────────────────┘
                    │
┌─────────────────────────────────────────┐
│   Check all burner isolation valves are closed  │
└─────────────────────────────────────────┘
                    │
┌─────────────────────────────────────────┐
│ Turn on gas - start gas boosters (if used) and prove operation │
└─────────────────────────────────────────┘
                    │
┌─────────────────────────────────────────┐
│ Energise weep by-pass system and prove downstream pipework is sound │
└─────────────────────────────────────────┘
           │                      │
┌──────────────────────┐  ┌──────────────────────┐
│ Set flue dampers,    │  │ Prove burner gas     │
│ by-passes etc,       │  │ pressure, not        │
│ and prove in purge   │  │ too high or low      │
│ position             │  │                      │
└──────────────────────┘  └──────────────────────┘
                    │
┌─────────────────────────────────────────┐
│  Initiate pre-ignition purge (5 x volume air changes) │
└─────────────────────────────────────────┘
                    │
* ┌───────────────────────────────────────┐
  │ Set air controls and flue dampers, by-passes, etc for first burner ignition │
  └───────────────────────────────────────┘
                    │
┌─────────────────────────────────────────┐
│        Introduce/energise ignition source │
└─────────────────────────────────────────┘
                    │
┌─────────────────────────────────────────┐
│      Open burner gas valve and ignite burner │
└─────────────────────────────────────────┘
                    │
┌─────────────────────────────────────────┐
│       Remove/de-energise ignition source  │
└─────────────────────────────────────────┘
                    │
┌─────────────────────────────────────────┐
│         Prove burner flame established     │
└─────────────────────────────────────────┘
```

In the case of single burner kilns:

Switch to process control

In the case of multi-burner kilns where additional burners are required:

Ignite subsequent burners (follow start-up sequence from*). On ignition of each subsequent burner, check that previously ignited burners are still alight

In the case of multi-burner kilns where no more burners are required:

Close air registers on non-firing burners (maintain sufficient air flow for fan control)

6

one for each kiln. Flues should lead to the outside of the building in as short and direct a route as possible, discharging above roof level. Long lengths of horizontal flue ducts should be avoided, especially with natural draught burners and those flues not fitted with forced/induced draught fans.

39   Flues are often provided with dampers. It should not be possible to completely close dampers controlling draught while fuel is reaching the burner. This can be achieved by cutting away part of the damper so that, with the damper in the fully closed position, one-third of the cross-sectional area of the flue remains open, or by fitting a stop which prevents the damper from being more than two-thirds closed. Dampers should be maintained in good working order and their operation checked regularly. British Gas publications IM 11[14] and IM 19[15] refer to this subject.

Safety controls

40   This section is a guide to the safe operation of fuel burners controlled by manual or non-programmable automatic control systems. Burner control systems should comply with appropriate standards, eg British Gas Code of Practice IM 30. Although applicable to single burner installations, BS 5885 also contains relevant useful information. Advice on the application of programmable electronic systems (PES) to fuel burner control is given in Appendix 3.

41   The control and safeguard requirements of any plant will depend upon its complexity. Where reasonably practicable, automatic or semi-automatic systems should be provided. Typical controls fitted to a continuous kiln are shown in Figure 4.

Safety shut-off valves

42   The fuel supply to all burners, including lighting torches, should be under the control of one or more safety shut-off valves. The number and type of valves relates to their throughput. Different types of safety shut-off valve are defined by their closing force requirements but they should close automatically. All electrically-operated valves should comply with BS 5963[16].

43   They should be interlocked with the flame detector (where fitted), fuel pressure switches and air pressure switch (where applicable), emergency/shut down switch and other safety monitors. Loss of signal from any of these should cause the valve(s) to close automatically.

44   Reopening of the safety shut-off valves should require manual intervention. A safety shut-off valve does not have to open automatically. It may, for example, be a free handle manual reset valve or a valve

incorporating a low pressure cut-off valve, provided it meets the appropriate closing force requirements.

45   The safety shut-off valve requirements do not relate to whether or not the plant is fitted with a flame safeguard system. They depend upon the way in which the last isolation valve operates as it opens to admit fuel to the burner to establish the burner flame. This last isolation valve can either be the burner manual isolation valve, or some other valve, for example, the safety shut-off valve.

Safety monitors

46   All exhaust and recirculating fans etc, essential to the operation of the burners, should have means for the direct monitoring of correct flow or pressure. Failure of any of these should cause de-energisation of the safety shut-off valve and lockout.

47   If excessive temperatures could result in unsafe conditions, an excess temperature monitor/detector should be fitted. The device should sound an alarm and de-energise the safety shut-off valve without manual intervention being necessary. If two temperature monitor/detectors are fitted, the first monitor/ detector at a lower temperature setting should, on operation, sound an alarm, while the second monitor/detector at a higher temperature setting should, on operation, close the safety shut-off valves.

Flame safeguard systems

48   A flame safeguard system, properly applied, can give valuable protection at all times and particularly during the ignition and warm up period. Such systems **should be fitted to all gaseous-fuel-fired kilns**, other than those of the types outlined in paragraph 55.

49   An essential part of the flame safeguard is the flame detector, of which there are two types:

(a)   ionising detectors - the ionising envelope of the flame will conduct electricity and rectify an alternating current passing through it. If this type of detector is to be used, those making use of the rectification property are recommended; and

(b)   radiation detectors - devices which detect the ultra-violet or infra-red radiation emitted by burner flames may be used. These should be kept cool and shielded from other detectors to prevent one detector interfering with another.

50   Whichever type of detector is used, it should be incorporated into a system which complies with the intent of BS 5885.

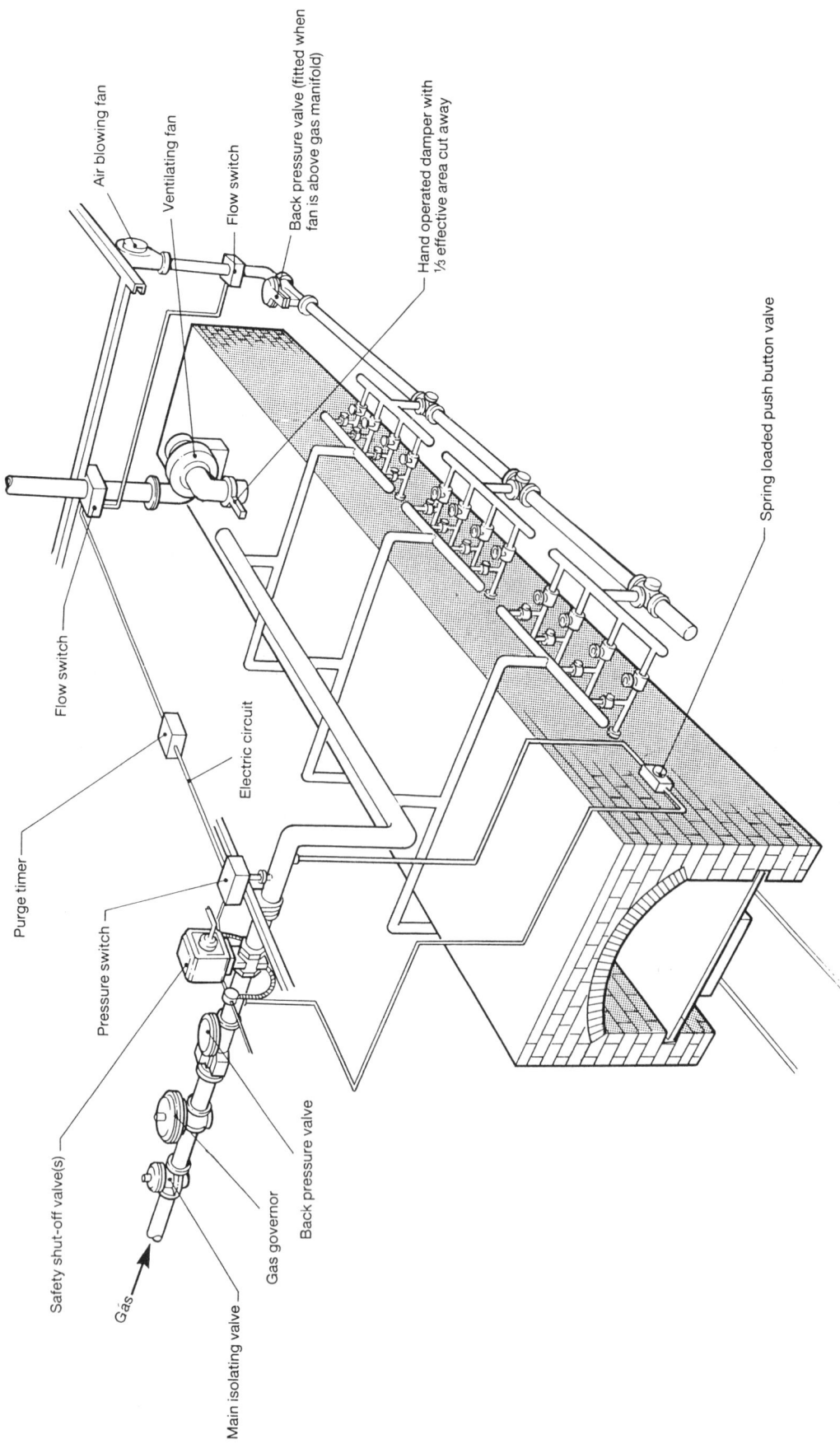

Air blowing fan

Ventilating fan

Flow switch

Back pressure valve (fitted when
fan is above gas manifold)

Hand operated damper with
⅓ effective area cut away

Spring loaded push button valve

Flow switch

Electric circuit

Purge timer

Pressure switch

Safety shut-off valve(s)

Gas

Main isolating valve

Gas governor

Back pressure valve

Figure 4 Gas fired tunnel kiln: layout of typical controls

8

51   The flame safeguard system should be arranged to shut off the fuel supply to the burner in the event of flame failure at the burner. Following a burner flame failure, a period of time sufficient to disperse any unburnt gas should be allowed before a burner can be re-ignited. Restoration of the fuel supply should require manual intervention.

52   The system can be fully or semi-automatic natural draught, but the burner control unit should comply with the intent of BS 5885. Whichever system is used, it should incorporate:

(a)   pre-ignition purge - of sufficient duration to disperse any accumulation of unburnt fuel before ignition; ie 5 x kiln volume air changes;

(b)   ignition - ensuring the maximum permissible energy release is limited to 53 kJ/m^3 (1.4 Btu/ft^3) of combustion chamber volume. **Also**, pilot ignition periods not to exceed 10 seconds and main flame ignition periods not to exceed 5 seconds;

(c)   flame proving - before the burner is allowed to remain in operation;

       and as an additional desirable feature;

(d)   burner post-purging on flame failure, of sufficient duration to disperse any accumulation of unburnt gas from around the burner before it is re-ignited by the kiln operator.

53   Any such burner control units fitted should be capable of continually withstanding the high temperature working conditions to which they will be subjected.

54   Light-up procedures should also include:

(a)   allowing sufficient time to elapse between consecutive attempts to ignite a burner to allow any accumulation of unburnt gas to disperse;

(b)   initial ignition of burners with **kiln doors open** whenever practicable. (In addition, if possible, burners should be opened to full flow, then dropped back to light-up flow to check flames are stabilised.)

55   A flame safeguard system may not be necessary on:

(a)   plant where the volume through which the combustion gases pass, ie combustion chamber, working chamber, primary flue, is less than 0.5m^3;

(b)   plant which has an enclosed combustion chamber of high strength, eg radiant tubes; and

(c)   those parts of a **continuous kiln of massive construction** which will retain heat (eg as in a brick-built tunnel kiln), and which run at temperatures above the auto-ignition temperature of the gas (eg 750°C for natural gas) for long periods (eg several months) - provided that during warm-up, continuous manual supervision is maintained.

56   However, burners used in pre-heat or similar zones, where temperatures can drop below the auto-ignition temperature, should be fitted with flame safeguards. The exception to this is some types of muffle kiln, whose construction makes the fitting of flame safeguards impracticable. In the absence of these safety devices it is **essential** to follow a safe light-up procedure and maintain constant supervision until the kiln reaches firing temperature.

57   A useful feature of the burners in firing zones similar to those described in paragraph 59, is the incorporation of a flame relay to give visual indication if a burner is extinguished.

Weep by-pass low pressure cut-off systems

58   A weep by-pass low pressure cut-off system, eg one complying with British Gas Code of Practice IM 20[17], should be fitted in the main gas supply pipeline to the kiln in cases where flame safeguard systems are not fitted, or where the gas supply passes through flexible pipes or swivel joints upstream of burner safety shut-off valves. In order to ensure the correct minimum flow rate of gas is passed, special attention should be paid to the size of the restriction orifice and the position of throughput controllers and other control valves, to avoid masking any open valves or leaks in the system.

59   Burners on continuous kilns particularly, may be arranged in manifolds, with the fuel supply to each manifold being controlled by a zone control valve. It is possible to pressurise the main safety shut-off valve weep by-pass low pressure cut-off system against the closed zone control valve, with some of the burner controls beyond the zone valve being open. One method of overcoming this problem is to provide a weep by-pass system or low pressure cut-off valve for each zone. A typical arrangement is illustrated in Figure 5.

60   In cases where no zone weep by-pass system is provided, greater reliance should be placed on proper training of operators and carefully controlled safe light-up procedure. As a first step, it is essential to ensure that all zone control valves are open before operation of the main safety shut-off valve weep by-pass low pressure

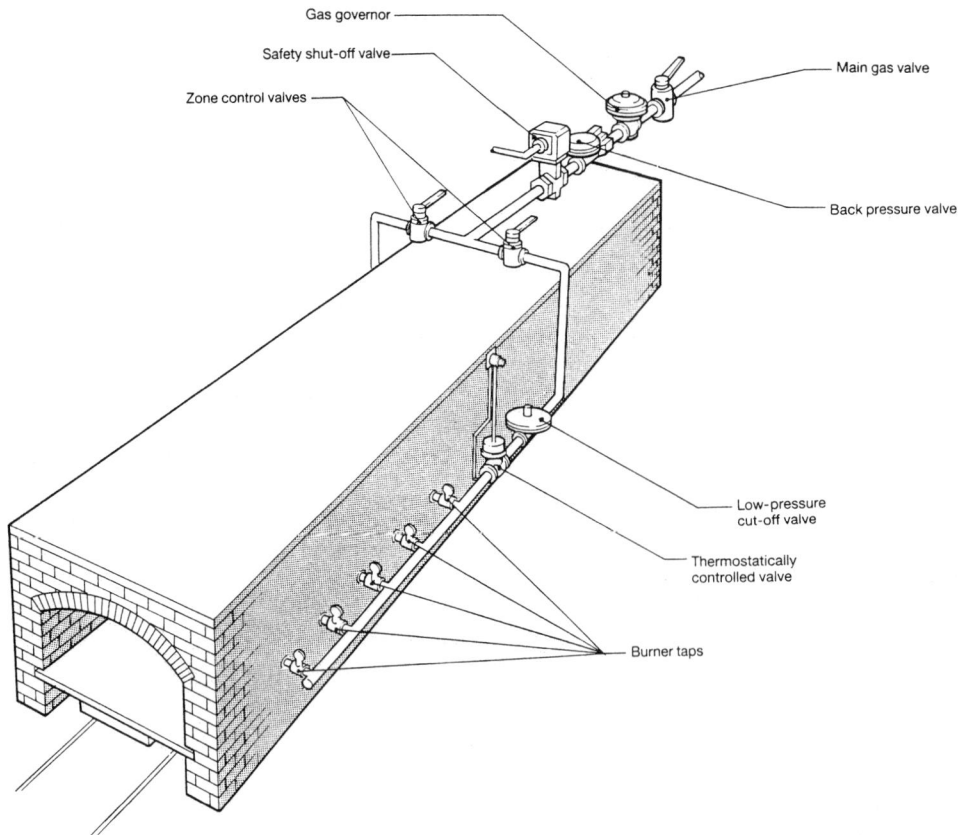

Figure 5 Continuous kiln: typical burner arrangement with low-pressure cut-off valves on each manifold

cut-off system. During operation, zone valves should be locked open.

Operating procedures

61   Clear and unambiguous operating instructions in a durable form should be readily available and there should be concise shut-down instructions displayed in a prominent position on or near to the kiln for use in an emergency, such as the example in Figure 6. This should include a warning to operators not to restart the plant without the full light-up procedure.

With all gaseous fuel-fired kilns, if abnormal problems are encountered, attempts to light the kiln should be suspended until the fault has been identified and rectified.

Shut-down sequences

62   The procedure to be followed during shut-down will depend on the process involved and the possible need to avoid excessive thermal stresses in parts of the plant.

63   In all systems, air supplies should be maintained until all pilot/main fuel valves and/or safety shut-off systems have been closed, and should further be maintained for a period to allow for post-run purging of the kiln. This is particularly important when a degree of fuel-rich firing has been in progress.

64   The safety shut-off system should be in the closed state when the plant is shut down and it should be

checked manually to make sure that it is closed.

65   Shut-down of combustion air fans, etc after safety shut-down or lockout is not essential.

66   It is desirable to leave the plant in a well-ventilated condition with main and burner fuel valves closed.

Explosion relief

67   For new kilns, manufacturers should take into account the possible risk of explosion and, if necessary, explosion reliefs should be fitted. Reliefs should be positioned so that they are unimpeded and do not present a risk to personnel if they discharge. Unless specifically designed to do so, doors would not be considered to act as the explosion relief.

68   For existing kilns, the need to fit any explosion relief would have to be assessed on a case-by-case basis. For further advice, the manufacturers or the Health and Safety Executive should be contacted.

ELECTRIC KILNS

Statutory requirements

69   The Electricity at Work Regulations 1989[18] apply to work with any electrical equipment. Their main requirements in relation to kilns are outlined in the following paragraphs.

70   All kilns should be provided with convenient means of isolation from the electrical supply and be protected against overloads and short circuit. The means of protection may be circuit-breakers or fuses, of suitable capacity for the circuit concerned. Apart from low voltage sensor wiring, all external conductors, ie wiring to the kiln and its control panel, should be suitably insulated and efficiently protected against damage, eg by enclosure in screwed metal conduit, by using wire-armoured cable or mineral-insulated metal-sheathed cable or, in the case of small kilns, flexible heat-resistant cable. All metalwork other than conductors should be effectively earthed.

71   The insulation of external wiring should be capable of withstanding the ambient temperature plus the temperature rise due to the load current. In warm areas, a heat-resisting plastic insulation should be suitable, but in hotter areas, special insulation or a mineral-insulated cable should be used. Reference should be made to relevant British or European standards specification. Terminals should be made from materials which resist corrosion when hot and be designed to remain tight when subjected to heat cycling.

72   For all types of kilns, the control panels or cubicles should be arranged and secured to prevent access to live conductors, except by authorised people. Such people should be trained and qualified electricians who, for the purposes of fault-finding or testing, may occasionally require a panel to be live while the doors are open. Doors on control panels should be capable of being locked, with other openable parts of the enclosure securely bolted on. The operator should not have to open any door or remove any cover exposing live conductors in order to make any normal adjustments.

73   Backs of kilns should be **kept secured in position.**

74   For detailed information regarding the electrical arrangements of particular kilns, users should contact the kiln manufacturer or the electricity board. The local office of the Health and Safety Executive may also be able to provide advice. Guidance on safe working practices is contained in HSE Guidance Booklet HS(G)85[19].

GAS FIRED KILNS
EMERGENCY SHUT-DOWN PROCEDURE

1.   *SHUT OFF* MAIN GAS SUPPLY VALVE

2.   *CLOSE* ALL BURNER GAS VALVES

3.   *INFORM* MANAGEMENT AND AWAIT FURTHER INSTRUCTIONS

4.   *RECHECK* THAT ALL GAS VALVES ARE CLOSED

DO NOT TAKE RISKS.

Figure 6   Emergency instructions for gas kiln

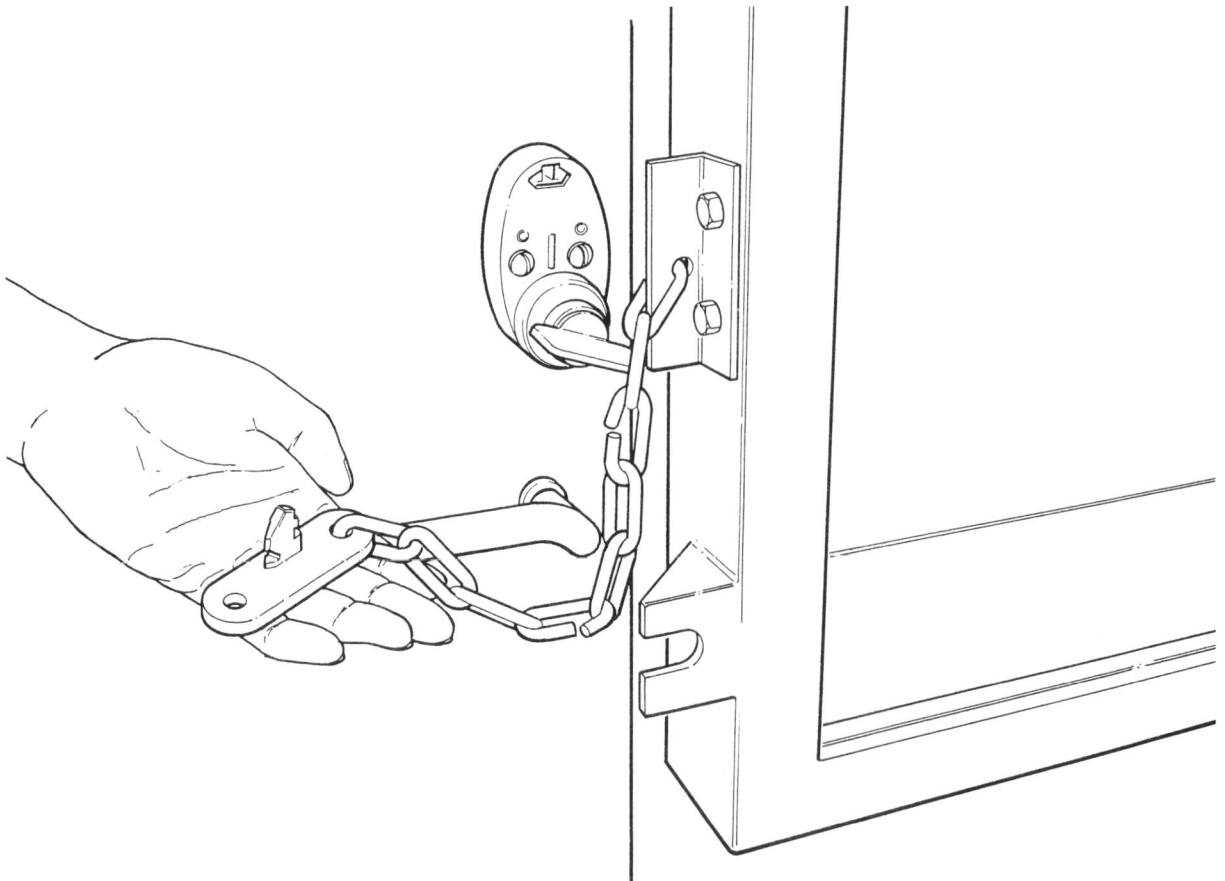

Figure 7 Unsuitable interlock

Interlocking

75   Advice on suitable methods of interlocking is given in BS 5304:1988 (section 9)[20], or its equivalent EN standard BS EN 292 Parts 1 and 2[21].

76   The accepted form of interlocking on kilns is by the use of trapped key or key exchange devices which ensure that the supply isolator is in the off position before the kiln door(s) can be opened, ie they should interrupt the power and not the control circuit. If other types of interlock systems between doors or covers and the electricity supply are used, they should be designed for positive operation to safety, ie the interlock switch is forced into the safe position when the door or cover is opened so that it cannot be wedged or stick in the on position.

77   If other forms of interlocking are used, they should achieve at least the same level of reliability and integrity as these methods.

78   The practice of connecting one part of the interlocking system to the kiln or kiln door by means of a flimsy chain as shown in Figure 7 is unreliable, easily defeated and unsuitable. A more robust system should be used such as that shown in Figure 8.

Precautions for intermittent kilns

Small oven-type kilns

79   These normally operate on the standard mains supply at 240 volts single-phase or 415 volts three-phase. The conductors in the sides of the kiln are usually of the open wire-wound type, accessible when the door is open, and a reliable interlock between the door and the electricity supply is essential, as described in paragraph 76.

Larger oven-type kilns

80   These also operate on mains supply at 240 or 415 volts and, in addition to the normal heating elements in the walls, usually have elements in the doors (with flexible connections). They may also have elements in the base of the truck. All external conductors, busbars and cables should preferably be completely insulated and efficiently protected against mechanical damage. If non-insulated busbars are used, they should be guarded and enclosed so as to prevent accidental short circuit by the dropping of tools or other metal objects onto them and to prevent people from touching them accidentally.

81   Connections to the doors or other moving parts should be by means of flexible cables. The live conductors should be enclosed in metallic braiding or

12

Figure 8 Example of trapped key control system fitted to electric kiln door

flexible metallic conduit; in either case these should be earthed and maintained in good condition. Metal conduit is not suitable to act as an earth continuity conductor and should be supplemented by a flexible earth continuity conductor.

82   Flexible connections at lower voltages (ie 110 volts or less) may, if the methods referred to in paragraphs 70 and 81 cannot easily be adopted, be of bare copper protected by enclosure in woven sheaths. Terminal boards should have covers.

Lift and moving-cover kilns

83   These kilns have heating elements in both base and cover, with flexible cables supplying power to the part which moves. Where applicable, precautions should be as for the large oven-type kilns.

84   Electrical interlocking should be provided to ensure that the supply to the heating elements in **both** cover and base is off whenever the base and cover are separated.

All types of intermittent kilns

85   It should not be necessary to change elements in intermittent kilns while a kiln is in operation, although testing of elements to check whether they are faulty may sometimes be required. If work on live conductors is

unavoidable it should only be done by authorised people (see paragraph 72), taking certain essential precautions as outlined in paragraph 88.

Precautions for continuous kilns

86   These kilns normally operate at 415 volts three-phase, so there should be no access to any conductors while these are 'live', except for essential work by authorised and competent people.

87   All external conductors, busbars and cables should be completely insulated and efficiently protected against mechanical damage. The heating elements may be arranged in sections, each with separate isolating switches. Fuse or circuit breaker protection should be provided for the whole kiln and for each separate section.

88   The changing of elements should, whenever possible, be done with the electrical supply to the kiln isolated or at the least, the appropriate section isolated. In this latter case, the authorised person should satisfy themselves that it is safe to work in that environment If the relevant part of the electrical system cannot be isolated, then live working should only be carried out by competent, authorised people working to an agreed procedure, having first taken steps to ensure that live conductors and earthed equipment are not simultaneously exposed within reach.

13

Precautions for fast fire kilns

89   As these are essentially tunnel kilns, there are no doors and therefore interlocks will not be fitted. However, the design should ensure that operators cannot, during the normal course of their work, accidentally come into contact with live heating elements and precautions for control panels, cables etc, and for safety during maintenance work would be the same as for other types of electric kiln.

MAINTENANCE OF PLANT AND SAFETY EQUIPMENT

90   Adequate technical information should be available for all plant and safety equipment to enable proper maintenance to be carried out. Such information should include electrical wiring diagrams.

91   If safety devices are to continue to operate satisfactorily and to provide the protection for which they are designed, they should be properly maintained, examined at regular intervals and (if practicable), tested. Advice on the nature and frequency of maintenance, examinations and testing should be sought from the manufacturer of the safety device or kiln and the suppliers of the fuel. Regular maintenance of other kiln equipment, such as burners, is equally necessary. If continued safe operation of plant and safety equipment is to be assured, all maintenance work should be carried out by trained and competent personnel using compatible spare parts. Anyone working on gas plant, should be trained in accordance with HSC Approved Code of Practice 20[22].

92   A written record of the routine servicing of safety devices and the results of examinations or tests should be kept. An example of a form of record is shown in Appendix 4.

Health risks

93   Some older kilns may have asbestos as part of the insulation. This should be borne in mind during maintenance, renovation or demolition work. Further guidance is contained in the CIAC booklet, *Asbestos in kilns and driers*[23].

94   Many kilns now contain, as part of their construction, man-made mineral fibres (MMMF), including ceramic fibres in higher temperature applications. MMMF materials have been assigned a maximum exposure limit (MEL) based on possible long-term health risks resulting from the inhalation of MMMF dust. Ceramic fibre should be considered to be the most hazardous form of MMMF. Effective precautions should therefore be applied, to ensure that workers' exposure does not exceed the MEL, and that exposure levels are reduced to the lowest level that is reasonably practicable in the circumstances.

Figure 9 Precautions for working with ceramic fibre within a kiln

95   MMMF materials should not pose a risk to kiln operators during normal work activities **but** when maintenance work is carried out which involves disturbing these materials, the potential for dust release and worker exposure arises. Working methods should be chosen to minimise the amount of dust created.

96   Where it is not possible to prevent the creation of dust, appropriate precautions should be taken. These may include local dust control measures and the wearing of suitable respiratory protective equipment and protective clothing as shown in Figure 9. HSE Guidance Note EH 46[24] gives specific advice and further guidance can be obtained from the local office of the Health and Safety Executive.

FIRE AND THE SITING OF POTTERY KILNS

97   A number of fires have occurred in potteries caused by overheated wood, which forms part of the construction of ceilings/floors above pottery kilns. Wood starts to degrade at temperatures as low as 80°C, and timber held at temperatures as low as this can cause a fire by a process of self-heating and spontaneous combustion. Higher temperatures for shorter periods can also start fires. These fires usually occur at night or early in the morning when there may be nobody on the premises.

98   The wood is heated due to one or more of the three different methods of heat transference:

(a)   convection - where moving air transfers the heat;

(b)   radiation - direct heating of a cool surface by a remote heat source without heating the air between, heat transfer increasing rapidly with increasing temperature and decreasing separation distance; and

(c)   conduction - direct heating of materials due to heat transfer through connecting materials.

99   It is important to check that any wood near to a kiln does not overheat, with particular attention being given to convective heating arising, for example, when kiln doors are opened to aid cooling, and where no protection has been provided. It is possible to measure the temperature of the wood by using a thermocouple inserted into a small hole drilled in the wood for this purpose. Preventive action will be necessary if this temperature is found to exceed 80°C. Factors influencing this temperature include separation distance, the orientation of the wood with respect to the kiln, the thickness of the wood, and the temperature of the kiln at the time of the hot air release.

Remedial measures

100   When potteries are being constructed, re-equipped, or where the enquiries outlined in paragraph 99 show that remedial measures are necessary, the following steps may be appropriate:

(a)   a thorough appraisal of the problem and the proposed solution to ensure that an adequate level of protection will be achieved;

(b)   seeking specialist advice from the local fire prevention officer and the local authority building control officer;

(c)   ensuring compliance with the Workplace (Health, Safety and Welfare) Regulations.

Wood replacement

101   The most obvious and effective solution is to avoid the use of wood, or replace it in the vicinity of the kiln and use non-combustible materials. This is only necessary where the wood is so close to the kiln that no hot air exhaust system can be fitted, or where insulation is unlikely to provide sufficient protection. It is, however, a more realistic solution when a pottery is being set up or undergoing refurbishment.

Hot-air exhaust system

102   A collector hood of sufficient size (with exhaust duct) positioned above the door, and dampers through which hot air can escape is the best way to protect woodwork from the effects of convective heating. Exhaust fans will not be required if the flue has a large enough cross-section, and a gradient of at least 25%. Care should be taken in the siting of exhaust ducts to prevent them causing overheating of any woodwork in their own right. The Building Regulations 1985, Part J[25], covers the correct installation of ducts. Where exhausted systems are used, the fans should operate each time the door or dampers are opened, and a clear indication of their failure should be provided. Controls for dampers should be clear and distinctive.

Insulation

103   Insulation alone may not adequately protect woodwork from serious overheating. Where, for example, hot air is released from a kiln operating at 500°C, insulation may well be a practicable proposition, but with a kiln temperature of 1300°C and kiln/ceiling separation distances of less than 1.5 metres, it is unlikely to be a successful solution. It will be more effective if an air gap is left between the insulation and the wood and where insulation is used, particular care

should be taken to ensure that it is impervious to air, and that it covers all the wood necessary. Fixings should not bridge the gap between the insulation and the wood.

Shielding

104   A simple metal shield may be used where heating is caused by radiation, or for hot air release from low temperature kilns (< 500°C) at heights greater than one metre above the kiln. Shields should not be directly fastened to the ceiling, but should have a clear, well ventilated air space above them. Plasterboard, or fire resisting insulating board should not be used to directly underdraw conventional ceilings. Any small gaps between sheets of such board should be filled in, eg by skimming over the surface of the board. Fixings should not bridge the gap between the shield and the wood.

THERMAL ENVIRONMENT

105   In spite of the generally high level of insulation fitted to ceramic kilns of all types, a certain amount of heat inevitably escapes into the surrounding areas. This can be a particular problem with modern fast fire kilns. In addition, kiln cars and kiln furniture as well as the ware itself emit heat into their surroundings after leaving the kiln. With fast fire kilns, the conveyor sytems carrying large amounts of ware can cause a significant temperature rise in the surrounding work areas. In these cases, thermal comfort and heat stress need to be considered and heat fatigue, due to people working for long periods in a hot environment, can be a problem.

106   The Workplace (Health, Safety and Welfare) Regulations require that the temperature in all

Figure 10   Measurement of relative humidity with digital hygrometer

Figure 11 Use of small winch to assist moving kiln car

workplaces inside buildings should be reasonable, that is, it should provide reasonable comfort for workers. An extreme situation is the one where personnel have to go inside tunnel kilns for the purpose of clearing a blockage or 'kiln wreck'. In this case, special precautionary measures will need to be taken. Advice is contained in the CIAC booklet, *Kiln wreck clearance*[26]. Further information on thermal comfort and heat stress is given in Appendix 5.

Remedial measures

107   The ideal remedy for problems of overheating is to reduce local temperatures, for example by erecting heat shields to reduce heat transmission and/or improving ventilation. In some workplaces, the building structure itself may make this difficult to achieve and the layout of adjacent working areas may need altering, or workers may even need to be relocated. If the nature of the work makes this impracticable, the length of time that workers are exposed to uncomfortable temperatures should be limited, eg by task rotation.

OTHER CONSIDERATIONS

Means of access

108   If operators or maintenance personnel need to work on the top of kilns, consideration should be given to the means of access. Fixed, rather than portable ladders are preferable and it may be necessary to fit walkways, edge protection or other means to prevent falls from the top of kilns.

109   Clear access should be maintained around kilns; tripping hazards should be avoided and care taken to distance other workers so that they are unlikely to accidentally come into contact with hot surfaces.

Mechanical hazards

110   Thought should be given to any mechanical hazards which may exist, for example, trapping points created by feed mechanisms or by moving kiln cars or transfer cars. Where kilns are automatically loaded and unloaded on a pre-programmed cycle, operators and other personnel should be prevented from being trapped and crushed by moving parts.

111   A combination of fixed and interlocked guards or barriers and safe systems of work may have to be incorporated to achieve an adequate standard of safety. In some cases, where more complicated plant is involved, the addition of trip wires, pressure-sensitive mats and audible or visible alarms may also be necessary. A European standard relevant to this aspect of safety is in preparation.

Ergonomic factors

112   The loading of ware, particularly very large articles or items placed in refractory boxes, and also the pushing and pulling of loaded kiln cars can pose a risk of injury to operators. An assessment of these risks is required by the Manual Handling Operations Regulations 1992[27]; this may reveal the need for mechanical handling aids, for example, a simple small winch can help in moving kiln cars as illustrated in Figure 11. The regular lubrication of car wheels is also essential to ensure smooth running along the tracks.

Lighting

113   An adequate standard of lighting, particularly around control panels, should be maintained[28]. Emergency lighting, in case of power failure at night, may also need to be fitted.

Noise

114   Some of the equipment associated with kilns, for example ventilation fans may be noisy. If a noise assessment shows that operators are being exposed to noise above what is known as the second action level (ie 90dB(A) averaged over an 8-hour working day) then measures will need to be taken either to reduce the noise at source, if this is possible, or otherwise to provide hearing protection. Further information is contained in the CIAC booklet on noise[29].

Fumes from kilns

115   During the firing process, fumes can be given off from kilns. These may contain, among other substances, hydrogen fluoride, produced by the effects of the heat on some types of clay body, or organic vapours from burning off covercoat from ceramic transfers.

116   In many circumstances, exhaust ventilation (extraction hoods) will need to be fitted to ensure these fumes do not adversely affect workers. This should be considered as part of the assessment of risks to health required by the COSHH Regulations[30].

APPENDIX 1 EC REQUIREMENTS AND BRITISH STANDARDS

1   European Community policy on the avoidance of barriers to trade requires member states to accept products meeting any of the standards accepted within the community, subject to the qualification that those products should meet an equivalent level of safety etc. To satisfy Article 30 of the Treaty of Rome (as qualified by Article 36) and for acceptance under Directive 83/189 EEC (which requires the notification of new technical requirements and places obligations on member states) the following statement of mutual recognition applies to all references in this guidance to non-harmonised standards.

2   Any reference in this guidance to an equivalent standard is a reference to:

(a)   a relevant standard or code of practice of a national standards body or equivalent body of any member state of the European Community;

(b)   any relevant international standard in (by a public authority of) any member state of the European Community;

(c)   a relevant technical specification acknowledged for use as a standard by a public authority of any member state of the European Community;

(d)   traditional procedures of manufacture of a member state of the European Community where these are the subject of a written technical description sufficiently detailed to permit assessment of the goods or materials for the use specified; or

(e)   a specification sufficiently detailed to permit assessment for goods or materials of an innovative nature (or subject to innovative processes) of manufacture such that they cannot comply with a recognised standard or specification and which will fill the purpose provided by the specified standard, provided that the proposed standard, code of practice, technical specification or procedure of manufacture provides, in use, equivalent levels of safety, suitability and fitness for purpose to those achieved by the standard, which it is expressed to be equivalent.

3   The burden of proof, where a standard is challenged on the basis of the proviso, rests with the enforcing authority.

4   In addition, the results of tests undertaken by testing houses in other EC states are to be accepted as follows:

The results of checks and tests carried out by the bodies and laboratories of other member states, including in particular those in conformity with EN 45000, will be taken into consideration where such results provide a level of accuracy, fitness and suitability for purpose equivalent to the results of tests carried out in the United Kingdom, and where such bodies and laboratories offer suitable and satisfactory guarantees of technical and professional competence and independence.

British Standards

5   Where British Standards are referred to in the text:

(a)   where a BS EN number is quoted, this is a harmonised EC standard;

(b)   where any other BS is quoted, a standard current in another EC member state which provides an equivalent level of safety is an acceptable alternative. In the case of design standards for equipment, this is an EC internal market requirement and such standards are referred to as "BS .... or equivalent standard"; or

(c)   any other equivalent national or international standard may also be accepted.

APPENDIX 2 TRAINING REQUIREMENTS FOR KILN OPERATORS

Initial training

This should cover the following topics for **each** kiln under the control of the kiln operator:

1   Ensuring written instructions on the use of kilns are available.

2   Knowledge of the position, function and setting of all controls.

3   Recognition and knowledge of the function of the safety devices.

4   Gas kilns - detailed knowledge of light-up and shut-down procedures and sequences.

5   Knowledge of the routine checks, adjustments, maintenance and repairs to be carried out and their frequency.

6   Recognition of faults and their prompt and accurate recording, reporting (where necessary), and follow-up.

7   Procedures for transfer of information at shift change-over and passing on instructions to other personnel.

8   Ability to cope with abnormal or emergency situations, eg power failure, kiln wreck, failure of safety devices.

9   Recognition of hazards in the working environment, eg obstructions, lack of space, noise, overheating, insufficient light, mechanical hazards.

10   Knowledge of handling techniques (manual and mechanical) especially for heavy loads.

11   Ensuring that personal protective equipment is available and used where necessary.

12   Appreciation of any additional special hazards and what to do about them, eg ceramic fibre, LPG.

13   **Also** - knowledge of company rules and procedures, restrictions on the use of kilns and limits of responsibility of the operator.

Refresher training

14   This should particularly cover the topics in points 2 to 8.

APPENDIX 3 APPLICATION OF PROGRAMMABLE ELECTRONIC SYSTEMS (PES) TO FUEL BURNERS

1   This Appendix applies when the safety features of fuel burners are either:

(a)   wholly controlled by a PES; or

(b)   controlled by a system which includes a PES as an integral component.

2   Whenever a PES is used within the control system of a fuel burner, an assessment should be made of the possible risks arising from its failure. The assessment should consider the effect of failure of equipment designed to maintain the burner in a safe state.

3   The following features of fuel burners are regarded as being safety related (this list is not intended to be exhaustive):

(a)   purging the kiln prior to igniting the burner;

(b)   the ignition period limits for both pilot and main burners;

(c)   ensuring that the flame is sustained;

(d)   monitoring the position of the burner fuel gas supply valves;

(e)   monitoring the emergency stop push button/switch;

(f)   ensuring that there is sufficient air for combustion and for purging the kiln of exhaust gases;

(g)   purging the kiln after the burner has been shut off;

(h)   monitoring the postion of the flue damper;

(i)   monitoring the flow rate of gases in the flue.

4   Fuel burners controlled by a PES should be designed to protect the kiln from the effects of a failure in the hardware (random hardware failures) **and** from the effects of errors in the specification, design, manufacture, installation and operation of the system (systematic failures).

5   The design of the fuel burner control system should be governed by the degree of risk associated with it failing in a dangerous way and should take into account the following principles.

Configuration

6   The way in which the PES and non-PES safety-related systems are combined to ensure that the fuel burner is maintained in a safe state should have the following characteristics:

(a)   the combined number of PES and non-PES systems which are each independantly capable of maintaining the fuel burner in a safe state, should be no fewer than the number of conventional systems previously used to provide the required level of safety integrity;

(b)   a single failure of hardware in a PES-based safety-related system should not cause a dangerous failure in the total configuration of the safety-related systems;

(c)   a software failure should not cause a dangerous failure in the total configuration of the safety-related systems.

7   The above may be achieved by:

(a)   the use of additional non-programmable hardware, eg the use of a proprietory safety monitor; or

(b)   the use of additional PES-based hardware of a different design (diversity); or

(c)   the use of additional PES-based hardware of identical design, **providing that** the design is well established and that there is extensive experience of reliable operation in a similar application.

8   The final configuration and the extent of diversity depends on the degree of risk arising from the application.

Reliability

9   This concerns the susceptibility of the system hardware to random failures in a dangerous way. The intention is that the overall failure rate of the control system should be no higher than that of a system based on non-programmable (conventional) equipment.

Quality

10   This concerns the procedures used in the specification, design, manufacture, installation and operation of the system. These non-quantifiable aspects of how 'good' the system is relate to precautions against systematic failures caused by, for example, errors or omissions in the specification of the control system, or by faults in software. Manufacturers and suppliers of safety-related control systems ought to follow a quality regime, eg BS 5750, in the design and manufacture of their equipment.

11   The quality assurance techniques required will be dictated by the reliability required for the degree of risk identified **and** by the way in which the PES and non-PES systems are combined to make up the configuration of the burner control system.

12   The configuration, reliability and quality principles should be applied to the whole fuel burner control system to ensure that risks are effectively controlled.

13   Further information on PES is contained in HSE guidance and EC standards[31-35].

APPENDIX 4 SUGGESTED CONTENT OF KILN MAINTENANCE RECORD

1 **Kiln identification**

Department/Area

Make of kiln
Identification No of kiln

2 **Safety device(s) to be examined**
(Examples only)

Electric kilns -
Interlocking of kiln door with mains electrical supply

Gas kilns -
Interlocking of safety shut-off valve with flame safeguard
Interlocking of safety shut-off valve with exhaust/recirculating fan(s)
Weep by-pass system

3 **Defects found**

4 **Continued use**

Can the kiln continue to be used with safety?

5 **If no defects found**

Date of next test(s)

Signature of person carrying out test(s)

6 **Action to be taken, if defects found**

(a) Immediately
(b) Within a specified period

7 **Follow-up action**

Signature of responsible person who has noted test report findings

Signature of responsible person after repair and retest, where applicable

Date

APPENDIX 5 CALCULATION OF HEAT STRESS AND THERMAL COMFORT

Heat stress

1 The Health and Safety Executive does not recommend any limits for heat exposure. However, in the USA, the American Conference of Government Industrial Hygienists have assigned threshold limit values (TLVs) for heat exposure, expressed in terms of the Wet Bulb Globe Temperature (WBGT) index where:

$$WBGT = 0.7 \, WB + 0.3 \, GT \, °C$$

(WB = Natural Wet Bulb Temperature °C and GT = Globe thermometer temperature °C (radiant temperature))

2 The WBGT index is a measure of the highest temperature at which people may be repeatedly exposed without adverse health effects. The value for the index, calculated from actual WB and GT temperature measurements, can be compared with standard published tables to give an indication of maximum recommended work periods.

3 The values in the tables are based on people who are fully acclimatised, fully clothed and with adequate water intake, being able to function properly without exceeding a deep body temperature of 38°C. They also take account of the work/rest regime and estimated workload, assuming that the WBGT value of the resting place is close to, or the same as, that of the workplace.

4 For female workers, figures would be reduced by 1°C to recognise generally lower sweat rates and by a further 1 to 2°C for people who are elderly or obese.

5 This approach is also used in ISO Standard 7243: 1989[36], which gives advice on both the measurement and interpretation of the WBGT index.

6 The standard gives further useful information about heat stress, particularly at the extremes of temperature which may be experienced when dealing with a kiln wreck. Further information is also contained in HSE Guidance Note EH 57[37].

Thermal comfort

7 Thermal comfort is a different matter from heat (or thermal) stress. The thermal comfort of people not subject to heat stress is the expression of their satisfaction or dissatisfaction with the conditions to which they are exposed. A person who is satisfied with the thermal environment does not know whether he or she wishes to be warmer or cooler; a person who is dissatisfied does know that he or she wishes to be warmer or cooler.

8 The reaction of a person to the thermal environment (ie their satisfaction or dissatisfaction) depends on the workload and in turn, their metabolic rate or the rate of body heat generation. It is also related to the rate of heat emission from the body which is governed by the natural air temperature, air velocity, water vapour pressure (relative humidity) and the thermal resistance of the individual's clothing.

9 Optimum air temperatures for thermal comfort have been derived for different combinations of air velocity, temperatures, workload and clothing from Fangers Comfort Equation, which can be used to predict a subjective "vote" for any given conditions in the neutral zone, on a 7-point scale ranging from cold or hot. It is known that humidity levels in range 30-60% relative humidity without extremes of temperature or air movement, have little effect on the feeling of comfort but that even so-called moderate temperature deviations from the optimum, can cause discomfort, irritability, fatigue, increased clumsiness and loss of concentration. Further information is given in ISO Standard 7730[38].

10 Accurate measurement of relative humidity can easily be carried out using a **digital hygrometer** as illustrated in Figure 10 on page 16.

11 Further useful information about thermal environment is contained in the British Occupational Hygiene Society publication, Technical Guidance No 8[39].

REFERENCES

1   *Guide to the Health and Safety at Work etc Act 1974* Guidance Booklet (L1) HSE 1990 ISBN 0 11 885555 7

2   *Management of health and safety at work* Management of Health and Safety at Work Regulations 1992 Approved Code of Practice (L21) HSE 1992 ISBN 0 11 886330 4

3   *Workplace health, safety and welfare* Workplace (Health, Safety and Welfare) Regulations 1992 (L24) HSE 1992 Approved Code of Practice ISBN 0 11 886333 9

4   *Supply of Machinery (Safety) Regulations 1992* SI 1992/3073 HMSO 1992 ISBN 0 11 025719 7

5   *Work equipment* Provision and Use of Work Equipment Regulations 1992 Guidance on Regulations (L22) HSE 1992 ISBN 0 11 886332 0

6   Industrial thermoprocessing equipment (draft) EC pr EN746

7   *The use of gas in industrial process plant* British Gas Code of Practice IM 30 1993

8   *The Gas Safety Regulations 1972* SI 1972/1178 HMSO ISBN 0 11 021178 2

9   *The storage of LPG at fixed installations* HS(G)34 HSE 1987 ISBN 0 11 883908 X

10   *The keeping of LPG in cylinders and similar containers* Guidance Note CS4 HSE 1986 ISBN 0 11 883539 4

11   *Code of Practice for the selection, installation and maintenance of electrical apparatus for use in potentially explosive atmospheres* BS 5345

12   *Coal Mines (Firedamp Drainage) Regulations 1960* SI 1960/1015 HMSO 1960 ISBN 0 11 100464 0

13   *Automatic gas burners* BS 5885 Parts 1 & 2

14   *Flues for commercial and industrial gas-fired boilers and air heaters* British Gas Code of Practice IM 11 1989

15   *Automatic flue dampers for use with gas-fired heating and water heating appliances* British Gas Code of Practice IM 19 1983

16   *Specification for electrically operated automatic gas shut-off valves* BS 5963 1981

17   *Weep by-pass pressure proving systems* British Gas Code of Practice IM 20 1983

18   *Memorandum of guidance on the Electricity at Work Regulations 1989* Electricity at Work Regulations 1989 HS(R)25 HSE 1989 ISBN 0 11 883963 2

19   *Electricity at work: safe working practices* HS(G)85 HSE 1993 ISBN 0 11 882081 8

20   Code of Practice for safety of machinery BS 5304 1988 ISBN 0 580 16344 X

21   *Safety of machinery, basic concepts, general principles for design* BS EN 292, Parts 1 and 2

22   *Standards of training in safe gas installation* Approved Code of Practice (COP 20) HSE 1987 ISBN 0 11 883966 7

23   *Asbestos in kilns and driers* CIAC free booklet IAC/L57

24   *Man-made mineral fibres* Guidance Note EH46 HSE 1990 (rev) ISBN 0 11 885571 9

25   *Heat producing appliances* Building Regulations 1985 Part J

26   *Kiln wreck clearance* CIAC free booklet IAC/L40

27   *Manual handling* Manual Handling Operations Regulations 1992 Guidance on Regulations (L23) HSE 1992 ISBN 0 11 886335 5

28   *Lighting at work* HS(G)38 HSE 1987 ISBN 0 11 883964 0

29   *Noise* CIAC free booklet IAC/L54

30   *COSHH:a guide to assessment* CIAC free booklet IAC/L62

31   *Programmable electronic systems in safety-related applications: Part 2 General technical guidelines* HSE 1987 ISBN 0 11 883906 3

32   *Use of programmable electronic systems in safety-related applications in the gas industry* IGE/SR/15 Institute of Gas Engineers 1989 (undergoing revision) ISBN 1367 7850

33   *Safety-related instrument systems for process industries (including programmable electronic systems)* Publication No 160 Engineering Equipment and Material Users Association 1989 ISBN 0 85931 089 2

34   *Functional safety of electrical/electronic/ programmable electronic systems: Generic aspects* Part 1: *General Requirements* (IEC/65A (Secretariat) 123 British Standards Institution 1992 (92/27672DC)

35   *Software for computers in the application of safety-related systems* (IEC/65A/WG9)

36   *Hot environments: estimation of the heat stress on working man based on the WBGT index* (2nd ed) International Organization for Standardization (ISO 7243) Geneva 1989

37   *The problems of asbestos removal at high temperatures* Guidance Note EH57 HSE 1993 ISBN 0 11 885586 7

38   *Moderate thermal environments: determination of the PMV and PPD indices and specification of the conditions for thermal comfort* International organization for Standardization (ISO 7730) Geneva 1984

39   *The thermal environment* BOHS Technical Guide 8 British Occupational Hygiene Society 1990 ISBN 09 0592738 9

Other useful references

1   *Flexible metallic hose assemblies* Part 1: *Specification for corrugated hose assemblies* BS 6501 1991

2   *IEE Wiring Regulations: Regulations for electrical installations* Institute of Electrical Engineers 16th edition Stevenage 1991 ISBN 0 08296510 9

Availability

For details of how to obtain HSE publications, see back cover.

British Standards and ISO publications are available from: British Standards Institute, Sales Department, Linford Wood, Milton Keynes MK14 6LE Tel: 0908 221166

British Gas publications are available from: British Gas plc, Industrial and Commercial Gas Centre, 139 Tottenham Court Road, London W1P 9LN Tel: 071 242 0789

HMSO publications are available from: HMSO Books, PO Box 276, London SW8 5DT Tel: 071 873 9090

Printed and published by the Health and Safety Executive
C30   11/93